First Facts®
Map Mania

If Maps Could Talk
Using Symbols and Keys

by Erika L. Shores

Consultant: Susanna A. McMaster, PhD
Associate Director, MGIS Program
Geography Department, University of Minnesota

Hi! I'm Ace McCaw.
I speak the language
of maps. You can too.
Come on, I'll show you.

Capstone
press®

Mankato, Minnesota

First Facts is published by Capstone Press,
151 Good Counsel Drive, P.O. Box 669, Mankato, Minnesota 56002.
www.capstonepress.com

Library of Congress Cataloging-in-Publication Data
Shores, Erika L., 1976–
    If maps could talk : using symbols and keys / by Erika L. Shores.
        p. cm.—(First facts. Map mania)
    Summary: "Describes map symbols and keys and how to use them to read a
map"—Provided by publisher.
    Includes bibliographical references and index.
    ISBN-13: 978-1-4296-0056-9 (hardcover)
    ISBN-10: 1-4296-0056-X (hardcover)
    ISBN-13: 978-1-4296-2880-8 (softcover pbk.)
    ISBN-10: 1-4296-2880-4 (softcover pbk.)
    1. Maps—Symbols. I. Title.
GA155.S56 2008
912.01'48—dc22   2006100037

Editorial Credits
Jennifer Besel, editor; Bobbi J. Wyss, Veronica Bianchini, and Linda Clavel, designers;
    Bob Lentz, illustrator; Wanda Winch, photo researcher

Photo and Map Credits
Capstone Press/Karon Dubke, cover, 14, 21
Corbis/London Aerial Photo Library, 16–17 (photo)
Idaho Airships, Inc./Leo A. Geis, 5 (photo)
Maps.com, 4–5, 6–7, 8, 10–11, 11, 12–13, 15, 16–17, 17, 18–19 (maps)
Peter Arnold/Carl R. Sams II, 8–9 (photo)
StarFighters76/Mike Leatherwood, 20

The author dedicates this book to Mike and Eddie.
Capstone Press thanks the staff at Memorial Library at Minnesota State University, Mankato, for
    their assistance with this book.

1 2 3 4 5 6 12 11 10 09 08 07

Table of Contents

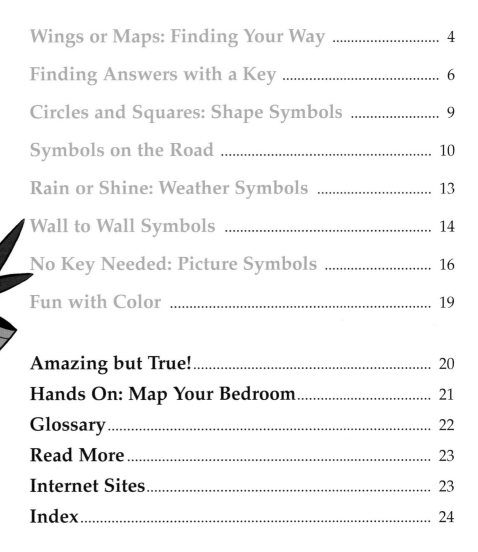

Wings or Maps: Finding Your Way

Where's the double water slide? If you were a bird, you could fly overhead to find it. But since you're not, you'll have to use a map. Maps use **symbols** to show where things are. That orange rectangle stands for the double slide. How did I know that? Read on.

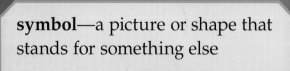

symbol—a picture or shape that stands for something else

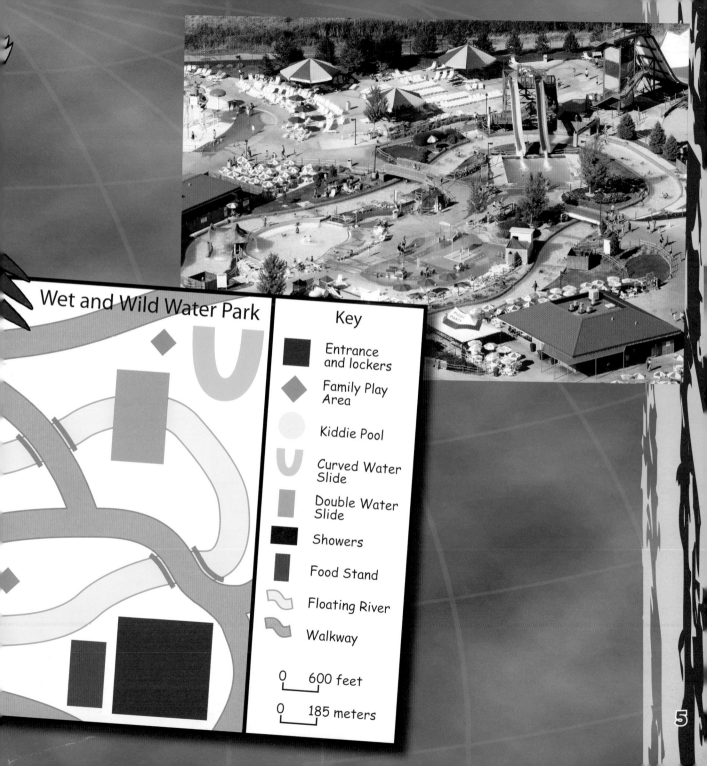

Wet and Wild Water Park

Key

- ■ Entrance and lockers
- ◆ Family Play Area
- ⬤ Kiddie Pool
- ∪ Curved Water Slide
- ▮ Double Water Slide
- ■ Showers
- ■ Food Stand
- 〰 Floating River
- 〰 Walkway

0   600 feet

0   185 meters

Finding Answers with a Key

You know how teachers have answer keys for tests? Well, maps have answer keys too. The box at the bottom of the map is the key, or **legend**. Use the map key to unlock the meaning of map symbols. So answer this: On this map, what do the squares stand for?

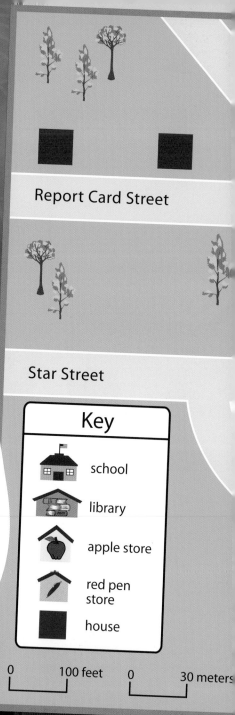

Report Card Street

Star Street

Key

school

library

apple store

red pen store

house

0   100 feet   0   30 meters

legend—another word for the key that tells you what the symbols mean

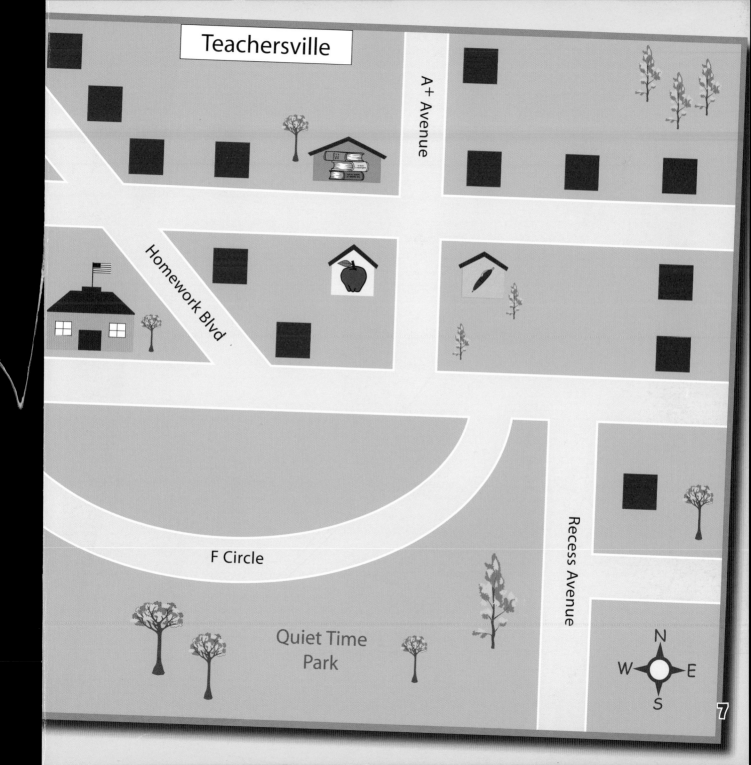

Teachersville

A+ Avenue

Homework Blvd

F Circle

Recess Avenue

Quiet Time
Park

N
W E
S

7

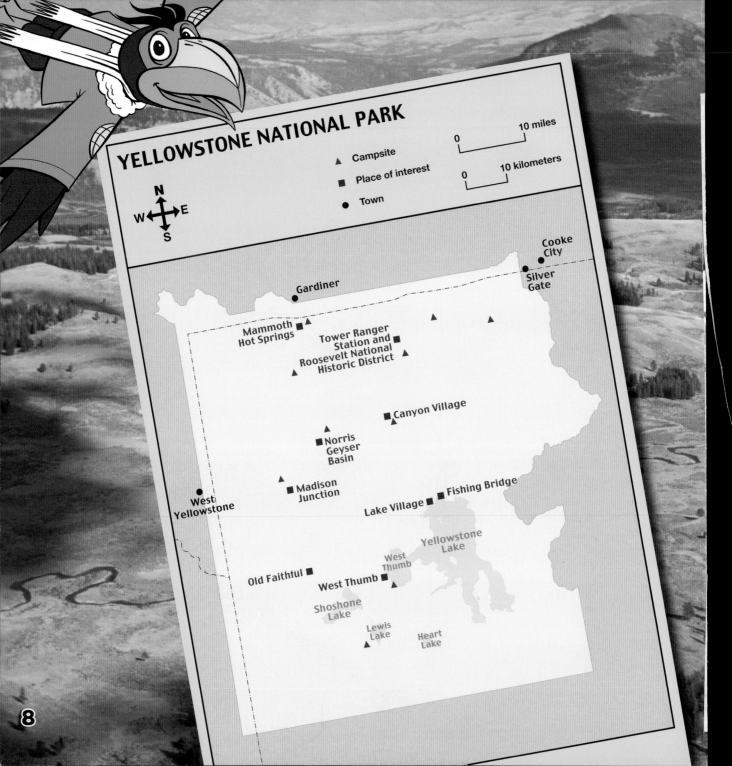

YELLOWSTONE NATIONAL PARK

▲ Campsite

■ Place of interest

● Town

0 ——— 10 miles

0 ——— 10 kilometers

N
W ✦ E
S

Cooke City

Silver Gate

Gardiner

Mammoth Hot Springs

Tower Ranger Station and Roosevelt National Historic District

Canyon Village

Norris Geyser Basin

Madison Junction

West Yellowstone

Lake Village

Fishing Bridge

Yellowstone Lake

West Thumb

West Thumb

Old Faithful

Shoshone Lake

Lewis Lake

Heart Lake

Circles and Squares: Shape Symbols

There are no giant red squares in the park. Why are there squares on the map? Oh, yeah! Mapmakers use shapes to stand for real things.

A square might stand for a building or a cool spot to visit. A triangle could be a mountain or campsite. Circles might be towns, planets, or bird baths! Use the key to figure out what the shapes mean.

Symbols on the Road

Symbols on a road map help drivers find their way. A symbol shaped like a shield stands for an **interstate** highway. Need some gas? Look on the map for the black circle closest to where you are. Black circles stand for towns. And where there's a town, there should be gas.

UTAH

Farmington

ARIZONA

550

40

Albuquerqu

NEW MEXICO

60

25

180

Silver
City

10

MEXICO

NEW MEXICO

⊗ Capital   〓⑩〓 Interstate

● City   ⦅54⦆ Highway

Map It!

What if you could travel to outer space? What might you see from the window of your spaceship? Draw a map of your space trip. Use shapes to stand for planets, stars, comets, or even aliens. Don't forget to put a key on your space map.

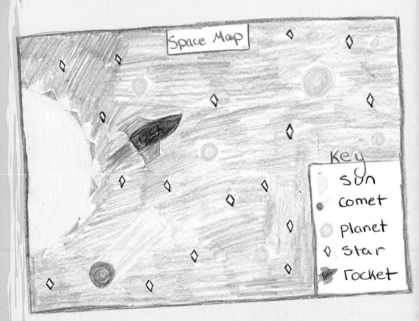

Space Map

Key
◇ Sun
● comet
◎ planet
◇ star
▲ rocket

National Forecast

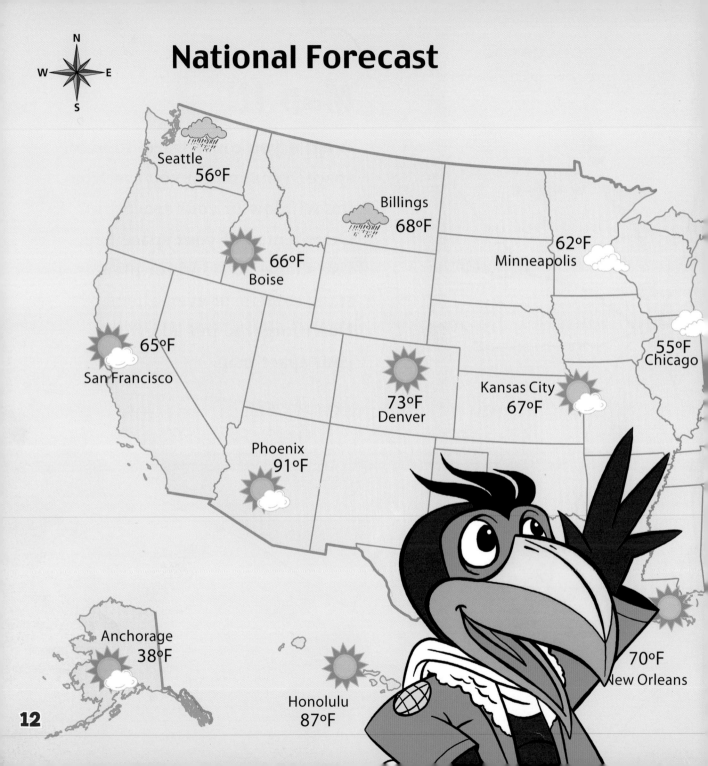

Seattle 56°F

Billings 68°F

Boise 66°F

Minneapolis 62°F

San Francisco 65°F

Chicago 55°F

Denver 73°F

Kansas City 67°F

Phoenix 91°F

Anchorage 38°F

Honolulu 87°F

New Orleans 70°F

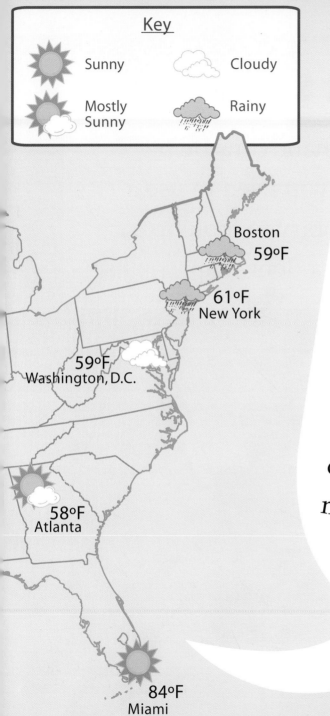

Key

☀	Sunny	☁	Cloudy
⛅	Mostly Sunny	🌧	Rainy

Boston
59°F

61°F
New York

59°F
Washington, D.C.

58°F
Atlanta

84°F
Miami

Rain or Shine: Weather Symbols

What will the weather be like tomorrow? Look at a weather map in your city's newspaper. Symbols on the map show the weather **forecast**. Orange circles mean sunny weather. Gray clouds with raindrops tell me I won't be flying.

Wall to Wall Symbols

Maps come in handy inside big buildings too. Say you need to use a computer at the library to look up a book on birds. Use a floor map.

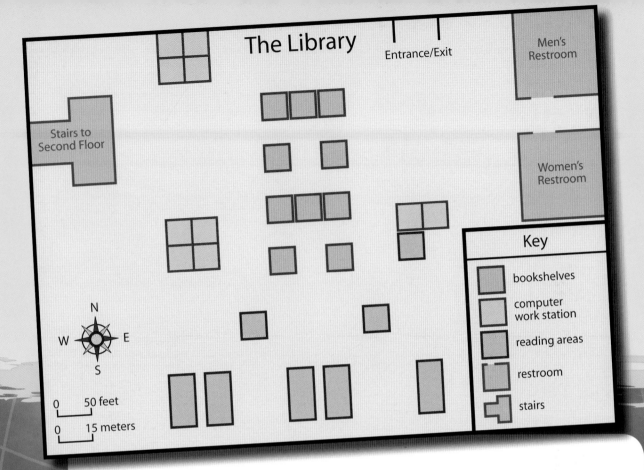

The Library

Entrance/Exit

Men's Restroom

Stairs to Second Floor

Women's Restroom

Key

bookshelves

computer work station

reading areas

restroom

stairs

N
W   E
S

0 — 50 feet

0 — 15 meters

A floor map isn't really a map of the floor. A floor map shows the **layout** of a place. Symbols show you where to find computers, stairs, and restrooms.

layout—the way things are placed in an area

No Key Needed: Picture Symbols

Most maps have a key. But there are some maps that don't have one. That's because they don't need to. These maps use pictures to show the real things they **represent**.

My favorite animal is the giraffe. Can you spy them on this zoo map?

London Zoo

N
W · E
S

0   250 feet

0   75 meters

represent—to stand for something

Map It!

Make your own treasure map. Hide a favorite toy in your backyard. Then draw a map to mark the hiding spot. You can use pictures of real things to show places in your yard. Give the map to a friend. Can they find your secret treasure?

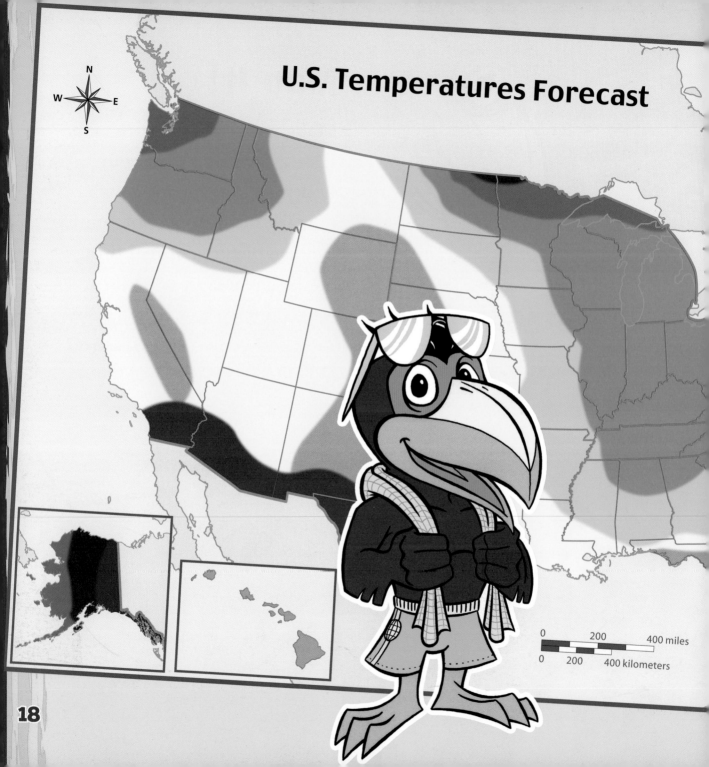

U.S. Temperatures Forecast

Fun with Color

Colors can be map symbols too. Temperature maps show how hot or cold it is. Red means it's going to be a hot day. If you live in Florida, grab your sunscreen and head to the beach. Symbols and keys can help you map out some fun.

Temperature

	10°F/-12°C
	20°F/-6°C
	30°F/-1°C
	40°F/4°C
	50°F/10°C
	60°F/15°C
	70°F/21°C
	80°F/26°C
	90°F/32°C

Amazing but True!

Sometimes, people need to know where the dragon sleeps or where the wizard lives. When? When they're playing video games. Gamers make maps to help them remember where things are in a game. They use symbols to stand for places and things. Sometimes, gamers put their maps online to help others beat the game.

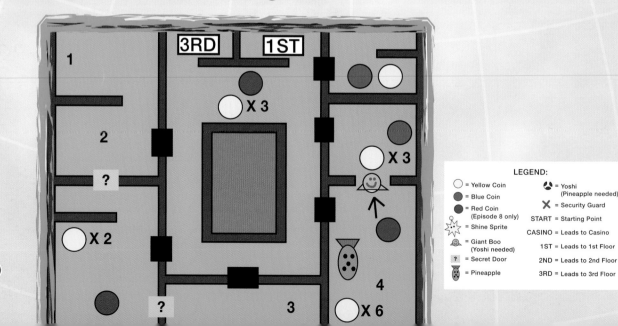

LEGEND:

○ = Yellow Coin
● = Blue Coin
● = Red Coin (Episode 8 only)
✺ = Shine Sprite
☺ = Giant Boo (Yoshi needed)
? = Secret Door
🍍 = Pineapple

🐢 = Yoshi (Pineapple needed)
✕ = Security Guard
START = Starting Point
CASINO = Leads to Casino
1ST = Leads to 1st Floor
2ND = Leads to 2nd Floor
3RD = Leads to 3rd Floor

Hands On: Map Your Bedroom

Just about anything can be mapped. You can draw a map of your bedroom. Symbols can represent your bed, dresser, windows, or toys.

What You Need

paper
colored pencils

What You Do

1. Draw a large box on the paper. The box will represent your room.
2. Next, look around your room. What will you include on your map?
3. Draw symbols to stand for things in your room. Draw a rectangle to represent your bed. Draw a small square to stand for your desk. What other simple shapes can you use to represent things in your room?
4. Draw a key in one of the corners of your map. Label everything in the key.

Glossary

forecast (FOR-kast)—a report of future weather conditions

interstate (in-tur-STATE)—connecting or between two or more states

layout (LAY-out)—the pattern or design of something

legend (LEJ-uhnd)—the words written beneath or beside a map to explain it; legends are also called keys.

represent (rep-ri-ZENT)—to stand for something

symbol (SIM-buhl)—a design or an object that stands for something else

Read More

Aberg, Rebecca. *Map Keys.* Rookie Read-About Geography. New York: Children's Press, 2003.

Chancellor, Deborah. *Maps and Mapping.* Kingfisher Young Knowledge. New York: Kingfisher, 2004.

Lomas, Susan. *Maps and Symbols.* Geography First. San Diego: Blackbirch Press, 2004.

Internet Sites

FactHound offers a safe, fun way to find Internet sites related to this book. All of the sites on FactHound have been researched by our staff.

Here's how:
1. Visit *www.facthound.com*
2. Choose your grade level.
3. Type in this book ID **142960056X** for age-appropriate sites. You may also browse subjects by clicking on letters, or by clicking on pictures anwords.
4. Click on the **Fetch It** button.

Facthound will fetch the best sites for you!

Index